Walt Disney®

VOLUME 1

ALPHABET A-Z

WALT DISNEY FUN-TO-LEARN LIBRARY

Aa

Alice picks apples and acorns on an autumn afternoon and gathers them in her apron.

apples

apron

acorns

Ape-king Louie plays acrobat and just misses an angry alligator.

ape

alligator

This book belongs to

_____

"Away we go," says Mickey, as his airplane follows the arrow.

Bb

Baloo the bear has a basket of berries in front and a bee in back.

berries

basket

bear

bee

bed

ball

bird

baby

book

bell

boat

Goofy reads a book to the
baby in bed, but the baby
wants to play with the ball.

Pooh rings the bell on the
boat while the bird keeps watch.

Dum-dum-de-dum! Doc plays his
drum for a dog, a duck, and a dragon.

Dd

dragon

drum

duck

dog

Dopey digs for diamonds every
day and loads them on his donkey.

diamond

donkey

Here are some picture stories. Can you tell what has happened?

A

Say the A words.

B

How many things can you find that begin with B?

C

Say the C words.

D

Say the D
words, too.

Ee

ear

Easter basket

eggs

Eeyore's ear tells him he got something extra in his Easter basket of eggs.

Eek! There's an elephant on this elevator! Look out, everybody!

elbow

elevator

elephant

Ff

Foolish Foulfellow the fox hides behind the flowers, but the Blue Fairy finds him.

fence

fairy

fox

flowers

fish

frog

Gg

Grandma Duck gives goodies to the goldfish in her garden pool.

gate

goldfish

garden

Goofy strums his guitar and makes the gorilla giggle.

gorilla

guitar

grass

Captain Hook hangs from a
helicopter high over the housetops.

Hh

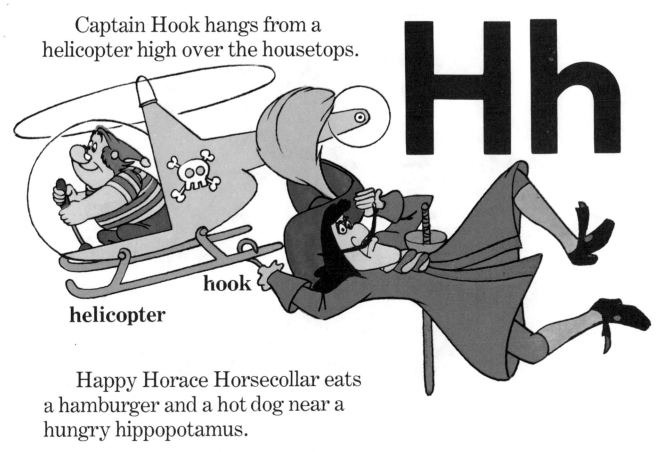

helicopter

hook

Happy Horace Horsecollar eats
a hamburger and a hot dog near a
hungry hippopotamus.

hippopotamus

hat

hot dog

hamburger

Ichabod Crane illustrates I with ice, ice cream, and ink.

Jiminy Cricket gets some help from the jack-in-the-box and jumps up to the table where the jelly is.

Jj

jack-in-the-box

jelly

Pinocchio has poured himself some juice from the jug. "Now where's the jelly?" he asks, looking at Jiminy Cricket's jacket.

juice

jacket

jug

JELLY

Here are some more picture stories. Can you tell what has happened?

E

Say the E words.

F

How many F words can you say?

G

Say the G words.

Say the H words in the picture.

H

Find the I words.

I

J

Find the J words, too.

JELLY

Kanga heats a kettle in the kitchen
while little Roo flies his kite.

kite

kitchen

kettle

kangaroo

leaves

Ll

Look out! The lion wants to lick that lemon-flavored lollipop! Louie leaps up a ladder to get away.

ladder

lion

lollipop

Lady brings letters to her lazy friend and lays them on her lap.

lamp

lap

leg

Mm

Mickey Mouse spent his money at the market on milk and mushrooms for supper.

market

money

milk

mushrooms

On the way home he met a magician who changed his milk into a monkey and his mushrooms into a mitten.

monkey

mitten

magician

That night, under a full moon, Mickey sat in a meadow and wondered how it could have happened.

meadow

moon

Nn

No noise in Never Land!
Tinker Bell is napping in a nest
of nuts.

night

nuts

nest

oar

octopus

ocean

Oo

O'Malley the cat often enjoys a ride on the ocean. But not today! An octopus is stealing an oar.

"Olives and oatmeal? How odd!" says Owl to Pooh. "I think I'll go home to my oak tree and have an orange instead."

owl

olives

oranges

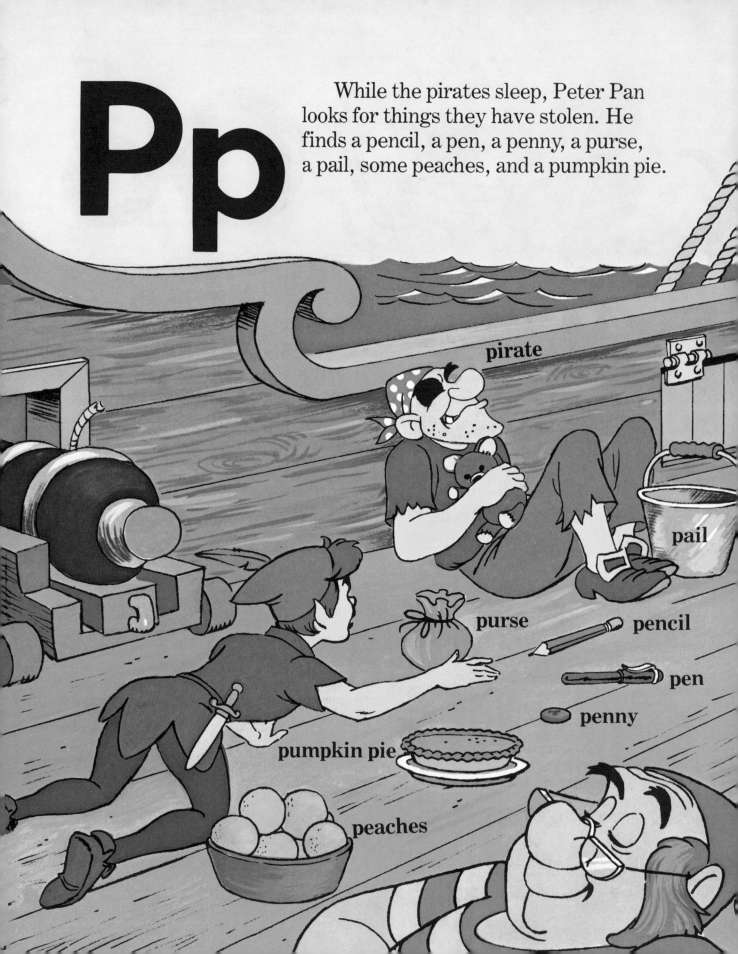

Pp

While the pirates sleep, Peter Pan looks for things they have stolen. He finds a pencil, a pen, a penny, a purse, a pail, some peaches, and a pumpkin pie.

pirate

pail

purse

pencil

pen

penny

pumpkin pie

peaches

Pluto and his puppy pal see a package on their pillow. What a pretty present!

Pinocchio paints a picture of his favorite foods — pancakes, popcorn, and peanuts.

Look at the picture stories.
What has happened?

K

Find the K words
in the picture.

Find the L words.

L

M

Say the M words.

N

Say the N words.

Say the O words.

O

Say the P words, too.

P

Qq

queen

The Queen of Hearts could not find the King. He was under the quilt, quietly drinking a quart of milk.

quilt

quart

Rabbit has a red raincoat to wear
when he roller-skates in the rain.
Watch out for that rock, Rabbit!

Rr

rain

rabbit

raincoat

roller skates

rock

raccoon

rope

roof

Robin Hood climbs a
rope to the roof to rescue a
runaway raccoon.

Ss

"What scrumptious soup," says Snow White, as she stirs in some salt. "Ah-choo!" says Sneezy. Salt makes Sneezy think of pepper, and pepper makes Sneezy sneeze.

salt

spoon

stove

soup

somersault

stairs

Snow White sits on the stairs and watches
Sleepy's super somersault. But he falls asleep!
Sweet dreams, Sleepy.

sky

squirrel

skunk

snow

snake

sled

skis

The skunk on his skis and the squirrels on their sled
make tracks in the snow. "Let me try," says the snake.

Tt

tree

"Look out for the terrible tiger!" calls tiny Tinker Bell as Princess Tiger Lily comes out of her tepee.

tiger

tepee

Tramp the dog finds a tired turtle on the train track and takes it away— just in time!

train

turtle

track

Uncle Scrooge sits under his umbrella and looks at his map of the United States. A unicorn peeks over his shoulder.

Uu

unicorn

umbrella

United States

Here are some more picture stories.
What has happened?

Q

Say the Q words in the picture.

R

Say the R words.

S

Say the words that start with S.

Say the T words.

T

U

Find the U words, too.

Vv

"Look here," Goofy shouts in a loud voice. "My van is full of surprises." He has a vest for Donald, a veil for Minnie, a vase for Daisy, and a violin for Clarabelle Cow.

van

veil

vase

vest

violin

Ww

Winnie-the-Pooh walks through the woods with a wibbly-wobbly wagon full of watermelons.

woods

watermelons

wagon

The wicked Wolf wears a wavy wig to fool the Three Little Pigs. But they know who is watching through the window.

web

water

window

wall

wig

wolf

Xx

X marks the spot on this pirate map.
That's where the treasure is.

Pinocchio plays the xylophone while
Figaro sings along.

xylophone

"Yippee!" yells Happy. "Watch my yellow yo-yo fly all around the yard!" Poor Sleepy. He yawns and yawns and yawns.

Yy

yawn

yo-yo

yard

Zz

zoo

zebra

"The zany zebra is my favorite animal in the zoo!" says Mickey.

Look at these picture
stories. Can you tell what
has happened?

V

Say the V words.

Say the W words.

W

X

Can you find
an X word?

Say the Y words.

Y

Say the Z words, too.

Z